Too Much Explanation Can Ruin A Man

Too Much Explanation Can Ruin A Man

Robert W. Crawford

David Robert Books

Published by David Robert Books
P.O. Box 541106
Cincinnati, OH 45254-1106

Typeset in Baskerville by WordTech Communications LLC,
Cincinnati, OH

ISBN: 1932339671
LCCN: 2004107410

Poetry Editor: Kevin Walzer
Business Editor: Lori Jareo

Visit us on the web at www.davidrobertbooks.com

"Winter Road" cover illustration by Dimitry Schidlovsky
dimitry.com

Contents

For my parents, Bill and Grace Crawford,
and my family,
Dina, Maria, and Alexa,
who, in so many ways, made this possible.

My thanks to the following publications (in alphabetical order) in which several of the poems in this manuscript first appeared or are scheduled to appear:

Compass Rose for "Across the Reach," "A Walk Home," "Maine Roads," "Trees from the Air," and "About Vermont"; *The Comstock Review* for "A Row of Stones"; *The Cumberland Poetry Review* for "French Braids" and "Not Ice-Out, Either"; *The Dark Horse* for "Town Roads"; *First Things* for "Olber's Paradox"; *The Formalist* for "Abiding," "Confession," "Cosmography," "Harbingers," "The Importance of Doors," "A Love by the Sea," "Not Necessarily You," "Power Failure," "The Road Agent," "There Has to Be a Reason for It," and "The Whole of It"; *Garden Lane* for "Chester Street," "A Modern Poet," and "Exposed"; *Iambs & Trochees* for "At the Top of the Stairs," "Stranger by a Window, Waiting for a Flight," and "When Boston Wins the Series"; *The Larcom Review* for "A Last Visit," "Passing," and "A Thing It's Not"; *Light* for "The Last Time," "The Love of One," "Marking Sound," "New England," "Projects," "Reincarnation," "Repetition," and "Walking Tour"; *The Lyric* for "Salisbury Cathedral," "To Unlearn Love," and "When November Really Ends"; *Pivot* for "Scattered" and "Weather Change"; *Rattapallax* for "In Florida"; and *Troubadour* for "An Abandoned Garden."

Town Roads

At each town line the old town roads change names
To take the name of where you're coming from:
The Chester Road will bring you into Derry;
Derry Road ends at the Chester green.
Confusion wasn't built in by design—
The roads were laid like spokes on wagon wheels
To serve the farms that long ago moved west—
But this arrangement's hard on travelers
Who simply want to get from place to place.
What these towns need is a Copernicus
To tell them that the center lies without,
And agencies to legislate that roads
That run between them share a common name.
And yet, when sitting on the bench behind
Two cannons and a monument to boys
Who went, when asked, to save that wider world,
But never came back down these wrong-named roads,
I see the possibility: perhaps
The towns were right. All roads don't lead to Rome;
They do, however, radiate from home.

The Whole of It

This first hot day, under an apple tree,
I feel you as a single drop of sweat
That slips along the middle of my back,
Along my spine, and traces me upon
Some magic paper that could take a man
And make him known, in no particulars,
Just known—as a land for its geography,
But where no valley, town, or mountain could
Explain the whole of it. I know, and yet,
This one wet fingertip of yours could map
Exactly what I am, and what might be,
And make each blossom hum above my head.

French Braids

While one hand is content to touch, admire
A balanced, careful weave—preserve for viewing
The beauty and the boundaries of desire—
The other hand is busy at undoing.
The quiet hand counsels restraint; afraid
To wreck the composition of composure,
It's wary of destruction just for fun.
The other wants to slip between each braid,
To tease apart the strands, let run, spill over,
Release, unbind, what was so neatly done.
Your urgent kiss decides which hand is played.
A gentle pull brings argument to closure.
Surprised, my hands attempt to catch your hair:
It falls the way the rain lets go the air.

The Road Agent

She stopped me just inside the door so I
Would know some news for me that couldn't wait:
"Just met a man you know—a Clarence Ward.
I was looking out the window when he knocked.
I was waiting on the flowers for the table,
For you to cross the field. It startled me."

"Strange hour for a visit. What brought him by?"

"He wants our vote for road agent this time."

"Well, it is the only job worth having here."

"Don't start. You like it here. Let me go on.
I didn't want to leave the window for the door
And must have had a frown when he began,
Because he took a step back off the porch,
And put his thumbs in his overalls, like this."
She did a perfect imitation of
The man whose farm is out on Fremont Road.
"He ended up too far away to part
With flyers on the things he'd do for less;
Just started in: 'Hello, my name is Clarence Ward,
And I'd like to be the road agent again.'
Said he 'knows the importance of a road done right.'
Truth is, I do believe he is sincere."

It was something about the way I know she turns
And keeps her head when the story isn't over.

"And that was all?"

         "I wish it was the end,
But the way he stood, and that earnest voice of his
So full of this concern for cracks and holes—
It may have been the way the light was falling
Behind him in the street, I just don't know—
It made me laugh."

         "You laughed at him out loud?"

And all I could think of was her laugh and how,
On some days, you know, of all the loves,
Why this one.

         She took the flowers from my hand.
"If you see Clarence, tell him I meant no harm."

A Row of Stones

In those December storms that start as rain
But end as snow, I try to count the flakes
As they begin to fall. But it's in vain.
I lack the dedication that it takes
To be a census taker of the snow.
I'll be distracted, as the tumult breaks
Across the field, by a long gray narrow row
Of stones, a wall within a stand of birch:
A thousand stones at least, pried, grasped below,
Pulled up and piled. In this hard springtime work,
The greatest effort spent to make the wall
Was lifting each the first inch off the earth.
I know when things get high enough they fall;
I'm struck in wonder that they're raised at all.

That Light

No longer near enough to overhead,
The sun seems bent on caring as it leaves.
The angle of retreating light divides
Each color and its shadow, making me
Abundantly aware of what it granted.
I see and hear much farther now these evenings:
I see the lower fields, the distances,
And all those things in need of gathering;
I hear the talk of neighbors closer to
The center of the town. And in this light,
If I can sit still long enough, I know
I hear you breathe, and see you raise your eyes,
Reflecting all my certainty of how,
Within this clarity, you call my name.

Exposed

I thought I could imagine, looking down,
The field had grown a little different from
The weight of us; the ground indented where,
Upon this hill, this grass—that blade still bent—
For just a kiss, we deserted all the world.
Looking up, I saw an open place
Less secret than the one that I remembered;
The eyes that would remark could see this spot
From an embarrassment of vantage points.
Our privacy had been a phantom thing.
Back then we hadn't cared who saw us, lost
To all the fields of view except our own.
I marveled at our heedless indiscretion.
I wished only to be there, exposed again.

Failure

If failure is the absence of perfection,
Is fall the failure of the spring to stay,
Or spring a failure in the fall's reflection?
These questions, gymnasts for a rainy day:
They tumble, twist and split, ask me to judge,
Compare, contrast each fault, and finally, trudge
Through words to score a point, for what it's worth.
But not today. The world is all temptation.
Have you (the *you* is so important here)
Been out to see the sky? I know it's marred—
Just another blemish on the earth—
But if you don't mind this tromping mess, still scarred,
Come join me for a walk. Let's watch it clear,
And hand-in-hand, in failure, find redemption.

By a Window

Upon a bed of chapel white,
Past curtains brushed in violet air,
The dalliances of evening light
Were gathered by the honey bee
And combed throughout your falling hair.
By a window open on the sea,
The loveliest gift, you gave to me.

About Vermont

They lived where you could see the maple sugar
Tap lines run down the hills to the valley floor;
Where the air held hints of wood smoke in July;
Where a dirt road was properly red on a map;
Where a boy and his friend were the only friends for miles;
Where the boy's mother wore a housecoat all day and talked
To the friend about romance novels and the one
She was writing by the stove, while in the barn
The father built an aircraft by hand that the boy
Knew by heart—like how far it could go before
It had to land on the other side of Jericho;
Where a boy knew every inch of that plane and that place,
And his friend learned fast about the intricacies
Of romance novels and flight.

Weather Change

At noon the night advanced across the west
And forced the sun to concentrate, and rest
On one last spot, a field against the sky.
Come, stand with me and watch the weather change.
It promises to wreck and rearrange;
Perhaps, pry out of me a lonely sigh.
Please, come with me. With you, I'd weather change.
And though it may seem difficult and strange,
A love of storms can be the greatest tie.

Abiding

Come sit with me and tell me of
Your sense of what is and isn't love.
Keep talking as we bide our time;
Keep talking; wile away the hours.
Though certain, sure, of reason's powers,
I'll listen for the slanted rhyme
That every hesitation makes
When calculating mortal stakes;
It is the lingering of an eye,
Or maybe the lingering of a sigh,
Or the lingering of a careless touch
That lingers there a bit too much.
I think I'll stay regardless of
What you say is and isn't love.

Not Ice-Out, Either

That thing! That thing! That awful moment when
You feel a person leave before they're gone.
I've known it too, as much as anybody;
Even with us, the few this side of the mountain.
You see, I saw the same thing happen when
Your wife was living with you. Down at *Mike's*.
Remember? You watched her as if she wasn't there.
I asked you, when she'd left, how it felt to be
That far removed from her in the same room.
And you said, I can still hear you saying it to me,
'Try living in the indifferent heat of green wood.'
It was that word 'indifferent' that stuck.
As if she didn't care. Or couldn't somehow.

That last year together must have been a hell,
But up to the end, you claimed it could be repaired.
Down by the railroad bridge, by the deep pool there—
While you were flailing the water for some trout—
You said to me, 'It's not completely dead.
Frigid? No, but not quite ice-out either.'
We can laugh about it now, and have another,
But can I ask you, for my own purposes—
Don't read too much into it, things are all right
With Annie and me; the spring is always hard—
When was it she became a ghost full-time?

The Importance of Doors

All she wanted was a door that she could close
To bound those cares too easily assumed—
Not nurse a grudge against them when she chose,
Or shut them out, as they had all presumed.
She promised more if given time to mend:
That given space, she wouldn't break, could bend.

For him, for them, it was more than just a door;
Some need they couldn't see, or saw with fear.
It was a revolutionary war.
They nodded 'yes,' did 'no' when time drew near.
The more she asked, the more they thought it theft;
And so, denied a little door, she left.

A Neighbor and Spring

So quick the snow is gone when winter dies,
Revealing all of fall's neglect for me
To rake and stack and sort, and drag away;
Its only saving grace, I get to clear
The corner of the yard where I can see
Your house between the cedars on the hill.

I look to find an open window there,
The sign that spring is really here to stay.
And if I do, I take my time, with care,
So when the linen curtains breathe aside,
I'll hear you play, again, the old piano,
Against the corner of that sun-lit room.

I'm never close enough to tell how well,
Or if with new-found joy you move the keys,
But that you play at all is good enough
For one alone with work to do on days
When half the world is coming back to love,
When half the yard still hides beneath the leaves.

Now spring again, it happened just today.
The window up, your music drifted out—
I heard it through the peepers and the brook.
It rose with all the new heat off the fields
And broke the clouds in pieces to the blue
That disregards the end of anything.

If I did get the chance, I'd tell you this:
If there were children here they'd feel it too.
Each tickled by the notes, in turn they'd run;
They'd run from tree to puddle, tree and back.
They'd laugh in time with music from your hands
And help me gather up all this debris.

Passing

We met against the foot of Cabot Hill,
Near three o'clock, in a sudden squall of snow.
Alone since I had shut Old French's gate,
I saw no need to rush a friendly greeting.

And he agreed.

He kept in silence down the path, while I
Kept coming up with something I might say;
If wishing could not make him go away,
I hoped that he could bear the quiet less.

I folded first.

"Bit cold?" I ventured to a hat, a face.
"Well," he slowed down a step, but didn't stop,
"Not all that bad a day for January;
The kids are still about on Higgin's Pond."

I nodded back.

Comforted by the thought that he had been
Where I was going, I began a question,
But he had passed, a careful distance formed,
And did not turn around to hear me start.

Then he was gone.

A cameo between the flecks of white,
He strode into the deepest part of winter:
Another ghost returning home that night.
I could have told him much about the way.

He didn't ask.

As I moved further up the path, and heard
The first faint filing sounds of skates on ice—
And felt again the sleep of buried woods
Not all that close to home—I was glad we met

In passing.

A Thing It's Not

He does deserve
What money bought:
A rural fling
That'll grow more rocks
Than native crops.
No lack of nerve,
He'll post his plot
To say, "It's mine,"
And hang a sign
That calls it a farm,
Because what's the harm
In calling a thing
A thing it's not?

New England

At noon the breeze blew hither
And cleared the lawn of leaves.
At one the wind went slack—
How calmly it deceives!
At two it turned to thither
And put them all right back.

When Boston Wins the Series

The throngs along the Esplanade;
The Charles crowded with light.
We'll be convinced there is a God—
This time, the world set right.

We'll feel the city roar in bliss
As we pass the Elliot bar:
Enough relief and happiness
To raise the evening star.

We'll find a place to rest our feet
Upon a Fenway stair.
You'll take my hand on Lansdowne Street,
Kiss me in Kenmore Square:

We'll see replayed that winning run
This patient town deserves,
And find, again, the sacred in
The geometry of curves.

Cosmography

Your new pajamas have these silver stars
That hang, precariously, in cotton blue.
You say that with the proper education
I might just find a falling one to view.
So, now, with this resplendent motivation,
I will attend a thousand seminars
To earn the astronomical degree
Appropriate for such cosmography:
I'll name each star, trace every constellation,
Map wondrously a Gemini or two;
Explore a universe of nights with you.

At the Top of the Stairs

You, stopping, laugh and whisper, "*War and Peace*
Can wait." You place my hand where it can run
Against your jeans, near skin untouched by sun,
And kiss me—any thoughts of reading cease.
My fingers concentrate in fold and crease:
The buttons on your jeans each come undone,
A fumble here and there, but, one by one,
Each one worked free—resistance and release.

Open at last, a dark blue denim vee
Still trembles on your hips and hesitates;
It needs a gentle push, a helpful hand,
To slip along your thigh, fall past your knee.
Across the hall, a turned down bed awaits;
The jeans can stay till morning where they land.

Not Necessarily You

You thought I read your poem with clinical
Detachment: coldly disregarding you,
The woman who wrote it. That's not quite true.

The poem is about a neighbor's horse,
And early mornings where the poem's *I*—
Not necessarily you—would talk to him
Across a yard—he, in a stable, *I*
Resting against a roadside fence—about
Loneliness. The horse would always nod,
Acknowledge that he understood the fears
That stopped the *I* from ever touching him:
The bar of private property; a wild
Belief that on the day she'd finally cross
The yard, with sweet red apples, he'd be gone.

You see, I read it well enough. But there's
Danger in going too far into a poem.
I focused on remembering it was
Not necessarily you who would have given
An apple, in your opened hand, to a horse
Who listened to the cadence of your voice
And understood the language of your body.

I kept myself to counting syllables,
Suggesting small improvements in the art,
Perhaps, because I, too, at heart believed
That if I'd crossed that yard you would be gone.

Solstice

To someone driving by I'd seem misplaced,
A man, or "country" silhouette design,
Propped staring at the constellations traced
Through shotgun holes in the crooked corner sign—
Our own Stonehenge, our winter solstice shrine.

But I'm just looking at my yard, the toys
Abandoned now at sunset for a chore,
And the shadow of a boy—before her voice,
"Please wear your mittens, Tom!" comes from the door;
Advice a father knows he will ignore.

Maybe I should pretend to be a beast
Ready to leap; make drivers brake, deduce
The danger here about to be released.
(I shouldn't think too highly of this ruse—
No one I know accelerates for moose.)

I'm tired of all these things I have to do;
Would that obligations ceased with flight.
Perhaps, to indulge myself and still be true,
I'll cross the road not looking left or right.
(No one is coming down this road tonight.)

The House at Night

I've overstayed. There's now a chance that they,
If looking out, might find me looking in.
The house, almost invisible by day,
At night, on snow, could stand for all that's been.
I haven't stopped to count their things (of course,
Some silver in a hutch, a book collection);
Drawn not by what light touches, but its source,
I'm looking for the shadows of affection.
I want a life within this narrow band—
So much for a wooden frame, a home, to hold.
The house at night becomes six windows, and
The light from the windows is the color of gold.
They have to be in love; they have to be.
I'll go. I'd need to live inside to see.

To Unlearn Love

Because love fails to gracefully retire,
I asked myself to unlearn love of you.
To disassemble and remove desire,
I'd unlearn love—a simple thing to do:
Tilt the soft earth with one firm step and send
A rising river back upon its source;
Reach through the air, through blue to black, and end
The endless circle of an orbit's course.
When I gave up, exhausted, I was left,
Unfairly, with my unlearned love of you
(I'd hoped to find it gone and cry out "Theft!");
A love, diminished, practical—and true.

There is a time when romance stills its chatter
And all, unknown, is known enough to matter.

Trees from the Air

The rivulets in the sand,
when the tide is going out,
look like carvings of trees.

And so, a man in love believes
that rain
washed trees from the air;

proving, once again, that even
the most beautiful of notions
can be wrong.

A Love by the Sea

In a fan-shaped chair beside the sand,
(With your long, lovely, careful hand)
You write and finger pages, glance,
As ocean and the shore romance;
An ambient motion to compose,
For some sweet purpose, we suppose.

The rhythms here urge all comply:
Some pressing need for the sea to try—
And the patient land to give it back;
It is not desire that they lack;
An eye to open and to close,
For some sweet purpose, we suppose.

But oh, for honor, never us.
A literary love it was,
A literary love remains;
It is the writing that sustains.
Unpicked, we shall describe the rose,
For some sweet purpose, we suppose.

Camo Cupid

The patient hunter's aim was true,
He needed just a clearer view:
He thought you were a willing doe
Beside her eager ten-point buck
And wanted one clean shot—with luck,
To let a single arrow go
To neatly pierce our two hearts through.

He must have blinked when you answered me.
Your human voice held back his hand.
Words that called for a second look
Revealed our forms had been mistook
And brought a "Hello!" from his stand.
Some things require certainty.
I guess I'm glad you said, "We'll see."

Across the Reach

The island had been his, but in a mood—
It turned out not to be a need—for more,
He'd sold it fair to a realtor named Jim.
Each morning, by the inlet bridge, he'd stare
Across the cold, receding gray of the reach
And track a lawyer's second home in progress.
Of course, they'd built the damn thing on the point:
Where the trail between the pines ran out, right where
She'd sat with him for hours to count the waves.
He'd watch, finish his donut shop coffee,
Crumple the cup, and go, with a shake of his head.

The Last Time

As they are sitting sipping lemon tea,
Sue leans in towards her friend Diane and shares:
"My William said the other night to me,
'To what the future holds in store I'm blinded.
I want to take it slow, not go too fast.
Let's make love like this day could be our last.' "
Diane lights up, "What passion! That he cares!"
Sue thinks a moment on her friend's reply,
Looks off across the lawn, "That's true, but Di,
One doesnt always want to be reminded."

Going Out

I have taken walks forgiven
And taken walks in blame,
But if I had to choose,
I'd take them just the same.

A Walk Home

For my sister, Cathy

Because the way from our town library
To Colin's house goes by my own, I found
Myself behind him on an evening walk.
He made a comic sight, all loaded up
With five large books that he kept dropping into
The kindling leaves already on the ground.

"Here, let me help."

            "Slippery jacket covers!"
He handed me a tome on sink repair
And *The Complete Collected Works of Shakespeare*
(But kept the heavier books by Stephen King).
"I like the plays, and now, with Jennifer
At school, I've got the time to read him through."

We walked a while in silence side by side—
As good friends walk—as true night fell unnoticed
Between the cradle house and Andrew's barn.
I, dwelling on the daunting gulf between
Myself and Avon's bard, was caught off-guard
When Colin, with a sudden sigh, confided:

"You know me well. I'm not a pessimist—
I still am fond of life—but, lately now,
I feel that my best days are all behind me."

"You're getting old; that's what it really is.
But name a day when this 'best' was had—one day
As good as Henry had at Agincourt."

He thought around our footsteps' fall, then said:
"It's strange the things that I remember now.
I saw it as we left the door of the church.
I turned to her and asked, 'Do you see that star?'
I'd never seen a star so bright before
Or since, so high in the southwest evening sky.
I was certain it would turn and be a plane,
But the color never wavered—white it stayed.
The frosted windshield couldn't keep it out.
It hung as steady as a Christmas story
When we arrived at the VFW hall.
It may be hubris, but we were marked for good."

We halted where the old town road divides.
I gave him back the books and had to smile
At his last question: "Have we said enough?
I must be heading right and home. Good night."

"Take care. Tell Anne-Marie I said hello."
I watched him go beneath Orion's rise
And stood reflecting on the simple fact:
Of all the gifts, the groom remembered best
A star.

Over the Edge

I like the maps
Where dark green flows
Over bunched brown lines
To a clear white edge.
I try to imagine
What's going on,
Just over that edge,
And on the other side:

I'd live there well
In a comfortable house,
Where from the porch
I'd know just where
The edge began,
And people peering
Over the map
Would have to imagine me.

In Florida

In Florida, when the wind is from the east,
There's bound to be a rainbow every day.
In Florida, in any kind of weather,
There's a billboard asking you to stay:

"All the amenities you ever dreamed of."

And so begins my dream of Florida:
A billboard asking me to dream about
A rainbow and a shower from the east,
In a gated place that has, without a doubt,

"All the amenities you ever dreamed of."

The shower beats on tiled roofs, falls into
The green green lawns that spread along the ground,
And breaks the surface of an azure pool,
Disturbing the reflection that I've found

"All the amenities you ever dreamed of."

And when the close-in sun returns, there is
A rainbow so beautiful I want to shout,
But can't, inside the gates, in Florida,
Where billboards tell you what to dream about:

"All the amenities you ever dreamed of."

And so it ends, with silence winding out
Between the eastern clouds like fishing line
At the end of the spool—violet line that reels
Away beneath a rainbow and a sign:

"All the amenities you ever dreamed of."

Attachment

A southern friend with a suntanned face
Called one November at our place.
He sat that night with a sweater on
And talked of sailing ships at dawn:
"It's amazing, Henry, what I've seen—
The weather blue, the water green.
I can't believe you'll just stay here
And bear the changes of the year."
Entranced, I thought I saw his view
And would have left to join the crew.
But out, just then, against the light
The last leaf tapped the window right.
"Yes, there's the difference between you and me,
I'll never make it out to sea…"
I didn't finish, but he knew—
He'd heard the leaf's deft knocking, too:
Attachment harder to explain
Than love in a late, cold autumn rain.

Maine Roads

On roads within the river's reach
There comes a careless turn on each,
Where you can see, below, the town.
I've often wondered what I'd find,
A parlor game of a certain kind,
If I took the exit, right and down:

Along with steam there ought to be
A red brick mill—a factory
That was built to last, that lost the fight—
On a River Street that's never far
From water and a corner bar,
By a rusting bridge, by a blinking light.

I'd settle there on a vacant stool,
Try not to look the foreign fool,
And when the snowfall comes that night,
I'd find a girl with auburn hair:
A girl who might take up the dare,
Deserving better, by her right.

We'd hear a distant whistle rise,
See glasses drained with weary sighs,
And talk in earnest of our plight.
I'd ask her then to leave with me,
To cross the bridge where we'd be free
Of limits, and that blinking light.

But when she hears the whistle blow
And glances at the snow that sweeps
Down empty streets while her town sleeps,
The girl will shake her head and say:
"A part of me so wants to stay,
Another me would surely go."

I'd like to answer to her fear—
Another me would surely care
Enough to stop and visit there—
But the road and I are in pursuit
Of other ends; the game is moot.
I understand you well, my dear.

Stranger by a Window, Waiting for a Flight

Entranced by all the sudden fires set
Along your neck—sunlight on fine gold hairs—
I went to Harborside with you and met
Your parents on the lawn. We put out chairs,
Drank gin, and, giddy in the ocean airs,
Played hearts. Near dinnertime, we made our bids
To be alone; kissed by the boathouse stairs.
We wed, made love (let down that hair), raised kids,
And summered there—until we hit the skids.
Things changed; they always do: you moved your head,
The sun moved on, and through half-lowered lids
I saw that you'd grow old and I'd be dead.
It was, exactly, what I always feared:
The years that were not years just disappeared.

Confession

That poem I said I wrote to God;
It wasn't.
I said it went beyond the flesh;
It doesn't.
Your speculation on the "you"—
Denied.
I told you that it was His touch;
I lied.
I thought poetic license safe;
I'm wrong.
It means what you suspected all
Along.
It's hard to hide in words from those
That hear;
Injustice done to both of you,
I fear.

Scattered

The change is so complete, who doesn't feel
October is a dream, November real?
One week, and we've forgotten paradise;
Accepted, as more probable, the facts
Of winter wind and ice: the proper price
The brilliant excess of the fall exacts.
We say we won't forget those days—the hue
Of maples that resemble fire. We do.

Stripped like trees in a slight, inconstant breeze,
We come to lose our grip on what we know,
Content ourselves with scattered memories:
Odd oak leaves left to crab across the snow,
The sound of children running out the door,
The things that disappear and are no more.

Walking Tour

Kipling, Rudyard; Beckett, Thomas—
The church floors here are crammed with tiles
That honor men who toiled and gave
Their lives for empire's haunting promise
Of privileged rest beneath these aisles
And praises sung well past the grave.

Your feet, in Britain, must take care;
There are dead people everywhere.

Millay's Child

Alkanet was the abortive Cora [Edna St. Vincent
Millay's mother] was searching for. Once she found it
in flower in July, she was able to use it to cause
Vincent to miscarry.
—Nancy Milford, *Savage Beauty*

I speculate on why you poisoned him
(or her, who knew?). You drank the alkanet
Your mother picked and brewed, not on a whim,
Or with lips forced apart by need, regret.
No, I suspect it had to do with beauty:
You feared—since Eros, your best muse, resigns
When Wednesday's play turns into Thursday's duty—
An interruption of your lovely lines;
You thought about that dressing table mirror,
Perceived your famous blush of hair defiled
With gray, a care-worn face, the wrinkles clearer—
Those mortal faults highlighted by a child.
You saw all ruined, the diminished stares,
And, ending it, returned to your affairs.

An Abandoned Garden

By August I noticed the lack of care,
And now in September I feel the despair;
The rusting tools, the vanished rows,
Reveal an all too brief affair.

The hopeful beginning has come to a close
As a meeting place for sinister crows
And devious weeds planning for when
They'll make this a plot where anything goes.

What kind of errant husbandman
Would let it fall to field again?
I think I know, I've met a few:
A fine egalitarian—

The type of man, a touch askew,
Who holds the universal view,
"To everything, a heart be true,"
But saves desertion just for you.

Power Failure

Groggy, at first, you think a bulb's burnt out.
But, the clock is off. The hum is gone.
An unfamiliar silence has returned.
Maybe it's just your room, but there's no water.
Maybe it's just the inn, but out the window,
Against the trees, the only light is the snow.
The valley down to Littleton is dark.
And so you wonder how far the failure goes:
This town; a few towns over; or did it start
Beyond the notch, spread all the way from Boston?
Because the silence seems so large, because
It's late at night, you wonder if there might
Have been a great catastrophe that changed
Everything on the other side of the mountains.
Though that would be an ugly, selfish thought,
Standing there looking out the window, and
Feeling the cold creep through the watery glass,
There is, engaged, a part of you—admit it!—
That wouldn't mind the starting all over again;
The desperate part of you that longs
For winter, and a covering of snow.

Marking Sound

The leaves, on a day, or two, decide to go—
Too many to regret a single one.
The apples, in a different manner done,
Snap off dead branches with a bump, then a blow;
They signal surrender, but grudgingly so.

A Modern Poet

In the wane of an expatriate's evening,
I found myself at the Expatriate's Inn,
Where conversation came from darkened booths,
And the barmaid wore the bare midriff of youth.

I touched the brim of my hat
In celebration when
Her warm browned belly brushed
The cool mahogany.

I resolved then and there
To live a life
Like a kiss on sunburned skin.

When she said, "Another?"
I traced a ring around
My glass of melting ice

In anticipation.

Harbingers

The wasps stumble; the days are more concise.
The apples fall, and the garden's yield grows thin.
Swamp maples and the weaker trees have turned
To fly the flags of new allegiance by
The lower pond that soon will be in ice.
The other, uphill trees, when they have learned
Of summer's abdication, will comply:
The changing of regimes is right on track.

Yet, I resist the revolution, swear
I could collect the harbingers that lie
In outlines of the coming drifts within
One pocket of this coat I'm forced to wear:
The leaves that fall are few enough that I
Can still imagine pasting each one back.

There Has to Be a Reason for It

"We don't sell many iron pots these days."
She turned the pot over to see the tag.
"That'll be twenty dollars even, Mary."
Putting it down she ran her hands across
The black rough edge and paused, expecting
A reply to tell her why this pot,
This Tuesday evening at the end of spring.

"Just add it on to Peter's store account."
Mary shifted her weight on the slanted floor.
It creaked—the same sound the trees make near zero.

Sarah retrieved the ledger from the shelf.
"It's been almost a year now, hasn't it?"

Mary checked how much was owed and signed.
"They diagnosed the cancer late in March.
She died June 10th. I started there in August.
So, yes, it's been a little under a year."

"And how is Peter coping with the loss?"

"If you were just to meet him on the porch,
You'd think that nothing's really changed at all;
He's still out every day to help his son,
Or tinkering in that cluttered barn of his.
You'd say he's fine. But it's strange. That's why I'm here.
When I cook something on the stove, he's said
A hundred times from his place at the table:
'Mary, there has to be a reason for it.
There was no sign; no sign you could have seen.
There are no other words for it than *struck down*.

She was just struck down.' And then, it's here, right here
He's always adding in: 'The only thing
Different was that damned aluminum pot!'
I know, deep down he thinks it's silly himself—
Lord knows, he eats up all the meals I make—
Still, the anger always startles me.
Of course, I tried to find another pot.
You'd think with all that junk around there'd be
A pot or two, so I could make a show
Of throwing the offending one away.
But there weren't any. None. I checked."
She paused, distracted by the notices
Above the humming lottery machine.
"I guess he needs to have a reason for it."

Sarah shook her head, "It was so sudden, though."
She reached to get a box.

                    "No need for that;
I'm parked close by out front. I'll probably
See you tomorrow morning for my coffee."

Mary picked up the heavy pot and left.
Almost at the car, behind her, she heard
The doorknob rattle as Sarah locked up early.

Clear Skating

On the ice of a snowless December,
Put your back to the wind and surrender,
Lift your arms in the air for sails,
Let go of the ground and glide:
A movement without details;
A moment along for the ride.

Chester Street

Mary,
The maples are orange and red.
The wind is around to the northwest now.
The morning's church bell ring is clear;
There'll be a frost beneath the stars.

Do you remember collecting the leaves?
We'd try to catch them as they covered the yard.
They made us dizzy when they filled up the sky.
The ones that got by us blew down the street,
Made a long scratchy sigh, and settled
As pilgrims near the church.

When children pass the parsonage
At the end of another day at school,
I watch them look over the graves
And hear them talk of Halloween.
It's then that I think I can see
You skip up the road with your books.

You named it best, "The Healing House,"
But it's not just this house, it is
This town: bright whites against the blue
In the middle, as if the world
With all its providence was centered here,
And falls away on either side.

I miss you most this time of year.
Enclosed,
            a crimson leaf I caught
From the oldest tree on Chester Street.

Reincarnation

The mysterious seals,
A gong's odd peals,
The grind of the ages in wheels.

They talk of perfection in circles.
They stare at polished spheres.
I think of perpetual cycles
And of preposterous gears.
I seek the comfort of arches;
A start, and an end, to my years.

Our evening fires,
My church of the shires,
The finality of spires.

The Love of One

Our heartfelt praise, in praise, is lost,
Like the first loop in a ball of twine,
Or one last inch of snow that's tossed
Upon a gathered drift of nine.
I guess it's our need to elaborate:
Bright lights on every tree are slung,
And wreaths in every window hung
When one upon the door would do.
The decoration's overdone.
We simply aren't content with few;
A thousand lights to celebrate,
Redundantly, the love of one.

Replaced

I love this place: the pitch of ground, each nook,
Mapped with the care of countless chores and walks.
The flowers know I feel, from just a look,
The burden in the bending of their stalks.
We have our private, if one-sided, talks.
They see I'm not the kind to run from ties;
The trees, though, are convinced it's otherwise.

No matter that I linger in their arc,
Or follow how each apple blossom globes;
That I can tell the difference in their bark,
The number, depth, and placement of their lobes,
And where and when they leave their autumn robes;
That I have asked no others for this waltz:
They whisper in the dark my claim is false.

I know between which limbs the sun will set
And where the moon will find each bough tonight,
But they know longing dreams, and of regret:
Earthbound, the trees can sense all thoughts of flight.
In storms they toss reproach that when it's right
I'll go; they say uniqueness is erased,
That they—despite my love—can be replaced.

Upon a Time

What if a wish came true,
But you that wished it so,
From waiting, found it woe?
The heart, astonished, knew
A distant, sad refrain;
The long awaited train,
An empty station through.

With Flowers

Out in a field with flowers, under grass.
In need of rain, the stalks break dry as glass.

The rye is high enough to hide my face
From passing glances cast along the edge,
But signs for careful eyes lead to this place;
I'm far from being lost, as they allege.

Pick two for tonight, five for the evening meal.
The flowers know I haven't come to steal.

I used existing paths, and doubled back—
A game of hide-and-seek to be alone—
But you could spot the freshness of my track,
And find just where I struck out on my own.

A vase is waiting on the kitchen table;
A tranquil scene, a pleasant country fable.

The storm clouds build against the northern range,
And in the film of dust the first drops stain.
Though I find I'm not expecting change,
I am, with flowers, reaching for the rain.

Projects

As long as he had a project or two—
The kind of work you could keep in view—
He'd pull his hat down by the brim
And keep the day ahead of him.
The tasks had middles but never an end.
He wouldn't look beyond the bend.
He wanted to say he'd kept his head
While making his way to the land of the dead.

Firewood

The maul, its task complete,
Splits one last log for fire:
A winter's ration claimed
Through use of gravity,
The oldest of desires.

The wood and I against
The season's first light snow:
All pieces of a store,
Paired to a block and shaped
By arcs that end in blows.

I know just where I am.
I'm curious as to why
My atoms came from sundered
Stars—the soot inside
The smoke of nebulae.

But the logs don't know what hit them,
And neither, here, do I.

Olber's Paradox

The heavens hold more stars than earth has grains
Of sand, and, given time, each tiny sun
Combined should make a world where starlight stains
The sky bright white, and dark would be undone.
And yet the night remains. The dim stars gleam
Their separate ways, and constellations drawn
Connect their dots, while under them we dream
And sleep, then wake to such a thing as dawn.
The universe, expanding since its birth,
Is larger, older than its light; sublime,
The force that keeps the constant day from earth—
The same that measures out our years—is time:
The limitation that provides us night
And saves us all from unremitting light.

Prayers

You cannot see a prayer
As you would notice
A rising cloud of breath
On the morning of the first frost,
But it surprises much the same.

You cannot see a prayer,
But there have been
So many prayers,
I think they fill the space
Between the stars,

And really are
As far as we can see.

The Swearing-in of Calvin Coolidge
Plymouth Notch, Vermont, 1923

Strange, the postman's loud, insistent knock
(The nearest phone, in town, two miles away)
Which roused them out of bed at one o'clock,
Tired from bringing in the August hay.
And stranger still, two telegrams they read
By lantern light: official ones, and both
With urgent news from Washington, that said,
"The President is dead. Please take the oath."
But in Vermont—where even summer skies
Can whisper that it's time to stack the wood,
And every breath on northern air implies
You're running out of days to do some good—
No one would be surprised, or think it odd,
To see a man look up and say "So help me God."

Repetition

The ground is covered in three feet of snow.
This is a landscape good for repetition:
Walk anywhere within the woods, walk slow,
Walk fast, try to escape the admonition
That "everything's been done before, you know."

A Last Visit

He died, but I still came to see for myself:
The effort greater than the distance crossed
In going up the walk of broken shale,
In passing flower beds with weeds (already!),
In asking help from a house to remember a man.

I went inside but left the door ajar.
Wearied by the threshold shadows, I sat
On the squeaky second stair and looked back out;
The house too quiet, small, and dark around
The door that framed the much desired light.

I saw the table set and him come in
With arms of evening wood for the stove, and us
Let in by his hand, just so, upon that door.
I heard him hang his coat up in the hall,
Which echoes if you listen by the steps.

What else was there to recall about a life?
The facts were in a strongbox in the den—
At the church we'd given them a decent hearing—
But if I learned anything in this house it's that
Too much explanation can ruin a man.

For all I knew, the truth was the good parts;
Yet, the end was harder than I imagined.
My heart, like wind in trees before the leaves,
Couldn't gain a proper understanding
Of what it came upon in early spring.

Salisbury Cathedral

I know my eye is drawn to be inspired
By flight on flight of arched and buttressed stone,
And though the height meets what the eye required,
The heart is not impressed by this alone.
The place their lord gave them to build this church
Was bottomland, a home for fowl and fog,
And not, by all rights, firm enough to perch
The tons of marble resting on this bog.
Defying calculation and good sense,
The mass and burden of the task appalls.
While I could understand if it relents,
I feel in me for earth to hold these walls:
The single spire celebrates, above,
Their faith the ground could bear this weight of love.

When November Really Ends

In April, when November really ends,
And the last suggestion of the snow descends—
With all else dragged to earth so long—I try
To see the newborn fingers of the trees
That barely scratch the surface of the sky,
And warm, again, to possibilities.

LaVergne, TN USA
02 December 2010
207075LV00002B/183/A